i-SPY

wildflowers

SPY IT! SCORE IT!

Introduction

The first flowering plants appeared on Earth some 200 million years ago and since then they have spread all over the planet. Not all plants produce flowers but as flowering plants are so adaptable to different conditions, they have become the most successful type of plant around. Ultimately, all animal life depends on plants: they provide the food we eat and the air we breathe.

As more countryside is built upon, some wild flowers have fewer areas in which to grow, so when you go out into the countryside, remember a simple rule:

'Take only photographs! Leave only footprints.' Hopefully, many other people will then be able to enjoy the wild flowers you find.

How to use your i-SPY book

Keep your eyes peeled for the i-SPYs in the book.

25 POINTS

If you spy it, score it by ticking the circle or star.

Items with a star are difficult to spot so you'll have to search high and low to find them.

If there is a question and you know the answer, double your points. Answers can be found at the back of the book (no cheating, please!)

Once you score 1000 points, send away for your super i-SPY certificate. Follow the instructions on page 64 to find out how.

15 POINTS

Wood Anemone

Scientific name
Anemone nemorosa

When does it flower?
March–May

Where is it found?
Open woods and hedges

What does it look like?
About 6–30 cm (2–12 in.)
tall with a white flower
sometimes tinged pink

White Water-lily

Scientific name
Nymphaea alba

When does it flower?
June–September

Where is it found?
Lakes and ponds

What does it look like?
Floating leaves with large,
decorative flowers

15 POINTS

3

Wild Strawberry

Scientific name
Fragaria vesca

When does it flower?
April–July

Where is it found?
Woods and shady roadsides

What does it look like?
Sprawling stems with long runners

15 POINTS

Woodruff

Scientific name
Galium odoratum

When does it flower?
April–June

Where is it found?
In woods

What does it look like?
Has bright green leaves edged with tiny prickles

This plant often grows in ancient woodland.

TOP SPOT!

25 POINTS

4

White Clover

Scientific name
Trifolium repens

When does it flower?
June–September

Where is it found?
Open, grassy places

What does it look like?
Low stems with three leaves

5 POINTS

Common Scurvygrass

10 POINTS

Scientific name
Cochlearia officinalis

When does it flower?
April–August

Where is it found?
Sea cliffs and along salted roadsides

What does it look like?

Lots of smooth, fleshy, heart-shaped leaves

Garlic Mustard

Scientific name
Alliaria petiolata

When does it flower?
April–July

Where is it found?
Open woods and hedges

What does it look like?
Tall, hairy stems with crinkled leaves which smell of garlic when handled

Do you know any other names for this plant?

15 POINT

Double with answer

Wild Radish

15 POINTS

Scientific name
Raphanus raphanistrum

When does it flower?
May–September

Where is it found?
Farmland and waste ground

What does it look like?
Tall with flowers that can vary in colour from white to purple, and sometimes from light orange to yellow

White Campion

Scientific name
Silene latifolia

When does it flower?
June–September

Where is it found?
Dry fields and roadsides

What does it look like?
Tall with sweet-scented flowers

10 POINTS

Greater Stitchwort

Scientific name
Stellaria holostea

When does it flower?
May–June

Where is it found?
Woods and hedgerows

What does it look like?
The tall flowering stems are four-sided and easily broken

10 POINTS

Common Chickweed

Scientific name
Stellaria media

When does it flower?
Throughout the year

Where is it found?
Farms, gardens, roadsides, seashores

What does it look like?
Sprawling and leafy with small flowers

5 POINTS

Wood Sorrel

Scientific name
Oxalis acetosella

When does it flower?
April–June

Where is it found?
Shady woods and hedgebanks

What does it look like?
Low-growing with leaves similar to clover

20 POINTS

Meadowsweet

Scientific name
Filipendula ulmaria

When does it flower?
June–August

Where is it found?
Damp meadows, woods and ditches

What does it look like?
Tall, upright and leafy

10 POINTS

Enchanter's-nightshade

Scientific name
Circaea lutetiana

When does it flower?
August–September

Where is it found?
Damp, shady woods

What does it look like?
Tall and single-stemmed with tiny flowers

20 POINTS

Cow Parsley

Scientific name
Anthriscus sylvestris

When does it flower?
May–June

Where is it found?
Woodland edges and roadsides

What does it look like?
Up to 1 m (over 3 ft) tall
with branched flower heads
containing many flowers
arranged in an umbrella shape

5 POINTS

Wild Carrot

Scientific name
Daucus carota

When does it flower?
June–September

Where is it found?
Chalky grasslands,
especially near the sea

**What does it look
like?**
Similar to Cow Parsley
although the leaves
are different

10 POINTS

Hedge Bindweed

Scientific name
Calystegia sepium

When does it flower?
June–August

Where is it found?
Hedges, woodland edges and gardens

What does it look like?
Twining plant with large, funnel-shaped flowers

5 POINTS

Ramsons

15 POINTS

Scientific name
Allium ursinum

When does it flower?
April–June

Where is it found?
Damp woods and hedges

What does it look like?
Clusters of star-shaped flowers. The whole plant smells strongly of garlic so that it is often called Wild Garlic or Wood Garlic

Daisy

Scientific name
Bellis perennis

5 POINTS

When does it flower?
Throughout the year

Where is it found?
Grassland including lawns

What does it look like?
A low plant with leaves arranged in a rosette

Oxeye Daisy

10 POINTS

Scientific name
Leucanthemum vulgare

When does it flower?
May–September

Where is it found?
Most kinds of grassland

What does it look like?
Like a big daisy

Greater Plantain

Scientific name
Plantago major

5 POINTS

When does it flower?
May–October

Where is it found?
Fields, gardens and waste ground

What does it look like?
A rosette of leaves from which the flower spikes rise up to 50 cm (20 in

Sun Spurge

Scientific name
Euphorbia helioscopa

When does it flower?
April–October

Where is it found?
Fields, gardens and waste ground

What does it look like?
The 50 cm (20 in.) stem ends in an umbrella-shaped flower head

20 POINTS

Common Nettle

5 POINTS
Double with answer

Scientific name
Urtica dioica

When does it flower?
June–September

Where is it found?
Woods, waste ground, hedgerows, gardens

What does it look like?
Tall, hairy plant with roughly triangular, saw-edged leaves

The young leaves are good to eat – True or False?

White Dead-nettle

Scientific name
Lamium album

When does it flower?
May–August

Where is it found?
Roadsides, waste ground,
hedgerows

What does it look like?
Similar to the Common Nettle but
with large white flower heads
and no stinging hairs

10 POINTS

Lords-and-Ladies

Scientific name
Arum maculatum

When does it flower?
May–June

Where is it found?
Woodlands, hedgerows and ditches

What does it look like?
The flower spike is shrouded by a
leafy cowl

*What is the other
well-known
name for this
plant?*

15 POINTS
Double with answer

14

Common Poppy

Scientific name
Papaver rhoeas

When does it flower?
May–October

Where is it found?
Farmland and waste or disturbed ground

What does it look like?
The tall stems are bristly while the leaves are toothed

10 POINTS

Red Campion

Scientific name
Silene dioica

When does it flower?
May–September

Where is it found?
Damp woods and hedgerows

What does it look like?
Similar to White Campion but red and unscented

15 POINTS

15

Common Valerian

Scientific name
Valeriana officinalis

When does it flower?
June–August

Where is it found?
Woods and roadsides

What does it look like?
Tall stems and tiny flowers in
dense clusters

20 POINTS

Scarlet Pimpernel

20 POINTS

Scientific name
Anagallis arvensis

When does it flower?
May–October

Where is it found?
Cultivated ground, roadsides and
sand dunes

What does it look like?
Small, ground-hugging plant

*Also known as 'Poor Man's Weather
Glass' because the flowers only
open in the sunshine.*

Bilberry

Scientific name
Vaccinium myrtillus

When does it flower?
April–June

Where is it found?
On heaths and moors and in woodlands on poor soils

What does it look like?
Thin woody stems with lots of bright green leaves

What colour are the edible fruits of the bilberry?

15 POINTS

Double with answer

Musk-mallow

Scientific name
Malva moschata

When does it flower?
July–August

Where is it found?
Open, dry, grassy and bushy places, often on roadsides

What does it look like?
Hairy stems topped with clusters of big pink flowers

25 POINTS

TOP SPOT!

Common Centaury

Scientific name
Centaurium erythraea

When does it flower?
June–August

Where is it found?
All kinds of poor
grassy places

What does it look like?
A basal rosette of pale green
leaves hugs the ground

20 POINTS

Ragged-Robin

Scientific name
Lychnis flos-cuculi

When does it flower?
May–August

Where is it found?
Damp meadows and woods

What does it look like?
As its name suggests, the
pink/red flowers have a
ragged appearance

10 POINTS

Herb-Robert

Scientific name
Geranium robertianum

When does it flower?
April–October

Where is it found?
Woods, hedgebanks, shingle
shores and mountains

What does it look like?
About 40 cm (16 in.) high
with hairy leaves and stalks

TOP SPOT!

25 POINTS

Dog-rose

10 POINTS
Double with answer

Scientific name
Rosa canina

When does it flower?
June–July

Where is it found?
Woods, hedges and
scrubland

What does it look like?
The bushes bear flowers
that are white or tinged
with pink

What are the fruits called?

Hemp Agrimony

Scientific name
Eupatorium cannabinum

When does it flower?
July–September

Where is it found?
In damp woods and on marshy roadsides

What does it look like?
Masses of tall stems topped by dense pink flower heads

20 POINTS

Cross-leaved Heath

Scientific name
Erica tetralix

When does it flower?
June–August

Where is it found?
In boggy heaths and moors

What does it look like?
Straggly, branching shrub with many small leaves measuring 2–4 mm (0.1–0.15 in.)

20 POINTS

Thrift

Scientific name
Armeria maritima

When does it flower?
April–August

Where is it found?
Sea cliffs and salt marshes

What does it look like?
Groups of plants form mat-like clumps and the pink flowers are sweet smelling

20 POINTS

Redshank

Scientific name
Persicaria maculosa

When does it flower?
June–August

Where is it found?
Roadsides, ditches, waste ground and cornfields

What does it look like?
Has reddish stems and usually a dark blotch on each leaf

15 POINTS

Common Restharrow

Scientific name
Ononis repens

When does it flower?
July–September

Where is it found?
In dry, grassy places

What does it look like?
Has a low, woody stem and small, downy leaves

 10 POINTS

Creeping Thistle

Scientific name
Cirsium arvense

When does it flower?
June–August

Where is it found?
Fields, roadsides and waste ground

What does it look like?
Masses of prickly stems and leaves

 10 POINTS

TOP SPOT!

Bee Orchid

Scientific name
Ophrys apifera

When does it flower?
June–July

Where is it found?
Mainly on chalk and limestone downland

What does it look like?
Like a big furry bumble bee visiting a pink flower

25 POINTS

Bramble

10 POINTS
Double with answer

Scientific name
Rubus fruticosus

When does it flower?
June–August

Where is it found?
Woods, roadsides, bushy places

What does it look like?
Has very prickly, arching stems and pink or white flowers

What is the fruit of the bramble called?

23

TOP SPOT!

Red Valerian

Scientific name
Centranthus ruber

When does it flower?
May–August

Where is it found?
Cliffs, quarries, walls and dry banks

What does it look like?
Grows in large tufts and has smooth, oval leaves and red, pink or white flowers

25 POINTS

Field Bindweed

Scientific name
Convolvulus arvensis

When does it flower?
May–October

Where is it found?
Farms, gardens, roadsides and by railways

What does it look like?
A trailing or climbing plant with funnel-shaped pinkish, reddish or even white flowers

5 POINTS

Lousewort

25 POINTS

TOP SPOT!

Scientific name
Pedicularius sylvatica

When does it flower?
April–July

Where is it found?
Bogs, damp woods, moors and heaths where the soil is acid

What does it look like?
Quite variable in height with double-lipped flowers

Cuckooflower

Scientific name
Cardamine pratensis

When does it flower?
April–June

Where is it found?
Damp meadows, stream sides, ditches, roadsides and mountains

What does it look like?
Flower head contains between 7 and 20 four-petalled flowers varying from white to pink

What is this plant's other common name?

15 POINTS

Double with answer

Common Mallow

Scientific name
Malva sylvestris

When does it flower?
May–October

Where is it found?
Roadsides, meadows, woodland

What does it look like?
The plant can reach heights of 1.5 m (5 ft)

10 POINTS

Red Clover

Scientific name
Trifolium pratense

When does it flower?
May–October

Where is it found?
Grassland

What does it look like?
It may be upright or sprawling with three-leaved stems

This is grown as fodder for cows and chickens.

15 POINTS

Selfheal

Scientific name
Prunella vulgaris

When does it flower?
June–August

Where is it found?
In grassy places and in open woods

What does it look like?
Oval, pointed leaves on fairly short stems

This has been used in medicine for hundreds of years.

Tufted Vetch

Scientific name
Vicia cracca

When does it flower?
June–August

Where is it found?
Roadside hedges, field and woodland edges

What does it look like?
A showy, pea-like plant that climbs using its tendrils

Common Vetch

Scientific name
Vicia sativa

When does it flower?
April–September

Where is it found?
Hedgerows, woodland and field edges

What does it look like?
A pea-like trailing or climbing plant with down-covered stems

20 POINTS

Purple-loosestrife

Scientific name
Lythrum salicaria

When does it flower?
June–September

Where is it found?
Damp areas such as lakesides, stream sides or fens

What does it look like?
Strong-growing spikes up to 1.5 m (5 ft) tall

20 POINTS

Rosebay Willowherb

Scientific name
Chamerion angustifolium

When does it flower?
June–September

Where is it found?
Waste ground, rubbish tips, disturbed ground, cleared woodland

What does it look like?
Strong growing spikes up to 1.5 m (5 ft)

This plant is also called Fireweed. Do you know why?

5 POINTS

Double with answer

Great Willowherb

Scientific name
Epilobium hirsutum

When does it flower?
July–September

Where is it found?
Woodlands, stream banks, ditches and marshes

What does it look like?
Bigger than Rosebay and with larger flowers at the top of the stem

10 POINTS

Heather

Scientific name
Calluna vulgaris

When does it flower?
July–October

Where is it found?
Heaths, moors, open woods and
boggy areas on acid soil

What does it look like?
A bushy, shrub-like plant with
spikes of small flowers

*It is also called Sling.
True or False?*

 10 POINTS

Double with answ

Bell Heather

Scientific name
Erica cinerea

When does it flower?
May–September

Where is it found?
On the drier soils of acid
heaths and moors

What does it look like?
The flowers are larger and
more bell-shaped than
those of Heather

 15 POINTS

Bittersweet

Scientific name
Solanum dulcamara

When does it flower?
May–September

Where is it found?
Damp hedges, woodlands and riverbanks

What does it look like?
It is a weak-growing, straggly plant that uses others for support

15 POINTS

Foxglove

Scientific name
Digitalis purpurea

When does it flower?
May–September

Where is it found?
Open woods, scrubland and hillsides on acid soils

What does it look like?
Tall, handsome spikes of thimble-shaped flowers

What organ of the human body is Digitalis used to treat?

10 POINTS

Double with answer

Stinking Iris

Scientific name
Iris foetidissima

When does it flower?
June

Where is it found?
In woods and scrub and on sea cliffs

What does it look like?
Thick tufts of evergreen leaves and bright orange seeds

Some people find the smell of the crushed leaves really unpleasant.

15 POINTS

Ground-ivy

Scientific name
Glechoma hederacea

When does it flower?
March–June

Where is it found?
Damp woods, hedges and waste ground

What does it look like?
This ground trailing plant has kidney-shaped leaves and it forms carpets where it grows. The leaves smell strongly when crushed

15 POINTS

Common Dog-violet

Scientific name
Viola riviniana

15 POINTS

When does it flower?
April–June

Where is it found?
Woods, roadside banks and grassy fields

What does it look like?
A low-growing plant with heart-shaped leaves

Red Dead-nettle

Scientific name
Lamium purpureum

When does it flower?
March–November

Where is it found?
Wasteland and cultivated ground

What does it look like?
Similar to other dead-nettles but with small, reddish-purple flowers

10 POINTS

Lesser Burdock

Scientific name
Arctium minus

15 POINTS

When does it flower?
July–September

Where is it found?
Open woods, hedges and waste ground

What does it look like?
A tall, bushy plant with heart-shaped leaves

Water Mint

Scientific name
Mentha aquatica

When does it flower?
July–September

Where is it found?
Bogs, marshes, lake and stream sides

What does it look like?
Upright plant up to 80 cm (32 in.) tall, smelling strongly of mint

15 POINTS

Spear Thistle

15 POINTS

Scientific name
Cirsium vulgare

When does it flower?
July–September

Where is it found?
Grassy places, by roads, waste ground

What does it look like?
Strong-growing plant with prickly, winged stems and spear-shaped leaf prickles

Green Alkanet

Scientific name
Pentaglottis sempervirens

When does it flower?
April–August

Where is it found?
On roadsides near gardens

What does it look like?
Tall, rough stems with
oval leaves

TOP SPOT!

25 POINTS

Viper's-bugloss

Scientific name
Echium vulgare

When does it flower?
May–September

Where is it found?
Chalk downs, shingles, dunes

What does it look like?
Tall, hairy plant with masses of
trumpet-shaped flowers

*This was once
used as an
antivenin for
snake bites.*

15 POINTS

35

Hedge Woundwort

Scientific name
Stachys sylvatica

When does it flower?
June–October

Where is it found?
Shady places such as woods and
hedgebanks

What does it look like?
Similar to a dead-nettle, with
broad leaves

*How does this
plant get its name?*

15 POINTS

Double with answer

Marsh Woundwort

Scientific name
Stachys palustris

When does it flower?
July–August

Where is it found?
In marshy places and on damp
roadsides

What does it look like?
Similar to Hedge Woundwort but
with much narrower leaves and
brighter flowers

20 POINTS

Musk Thistle

Scientific name
Carduus nutans

When does it flower?
June–August

Where is it found?
In grassy and bushy places

What does it look like?
Has spiny stems and big, drooping flower-heads

TOP SPOT!

25 POINTS

Betony

Scientific name
Stachys officinalis

When does it flower?
June–August

Where is it found?
In open grassy and bushy places

What does it look like?
Has slightly hairy, oblong leaves

20 POINTS

Pyramidal Orchid

Scientific name
Anacamptis pyramidalis

When does it flower?
July–August

Where is it found?
In chalk grassland and on sand dunes

What does it look like?
The thin stems are topped by a dome-shaped mass of flowers

25 POINTS

Southern Marsh-orchid

Scientific name
Dactylorhiza praetermissa

When does it flower?
June–July

Where is it found?
In open marshy places

What does it look like?
Has a stout stem and bright green shiny leaves, sometimes spotted

25 POINTS

Wild Thyme

Scientific name
Thymus polytrichus

When does it flower?
April–September

Where is it found?
Dry grassland, heaths, dunes

What does it look like?
Ground-hugging plant
that smells of the herb
when crushed

20 POINTS

Wild Teasel

Scientific name
Dipsacus fullonum

When does it flower?
July–August

Where is it found?
Waste ground, open woods,
riverbanks

What does it look like?
Strongly growing, large
plant with prickly
flower heads

15 POINTS

Black Horehound

Scientific name
Ballota nigra

When does it flower?
June–August

Where is it found?
In hedgebanks and bushy places, often near houses

What does it look like?
A bushy, weedy plant with a strong, unpleasant smell

20 POINTS

TOP SPOT!

Early Purple Orchid

Scientific name
Orchis mascula

When does it flower?
April–June

Where is it found?
Chalky woods, downs and sea cliffs

What does it look like?
A typical orchid with the rosette of leaves spotted in a purplish colour

25 POINTS

Meadow Crane's-bill

Scientific name
Geranium pratense

When does it flower?
May–August

Where is it found?
Roadsides, hedgerows, edges of
grassy meadows

What does it look like?
Strongly growing plant with deeply
divided leaves

How does the
plant get its name?

15 POINTS

Double with answer

TOP
SPOT!

Sheep's-bit

Scientific name
Jasione montana

When does it flower?
May–July

Where is it found?
On acid soils, on heaths, moors,
grassy roadsides, cliffs and shingle

What does it look like?
Fairly low, wiry stems
topped with blue
'pom-pom'
flower heads

25 POINTS

Germander Speedwell

Scientific name
Veronica chamaedrys

When does it flower?
April–July

Where is it found?
Grassland, hedges, roadsides, open woodland

What does it look like?
The stems grow along the ground at first before reaching upwards

15 POINTS

Heath Speedwell

Scientific name
Veronica officinalis

When does it flower?
May–August

Where is it found?
On grassy heaths and moors

What does it look like?
Creeping, hairy stems and leaves with erect flower spikes

15 POINTS

Bugle

15 POINTS

Scientific name
Ajuga reptans

When does it flower?
May–June

Where is it found?
Damp grassland and
woodland clearings

What does it look like?
The stems are hairy on
two opposite sides and the
flowers appear in rings
around the stem

Harebell

Scientific name
Campanula rotundifolia

When does it flower?
August–September

Where is it found?
Dry, chalky grassland

What does it look like?
Nodding thin stalks, thin leaves
and bell-shaped flowers

15 POINTS

Chicory

Scientific name
Cichorium intybus

When does it flower?
June–September

Where is it found?
Roadsides, grassy places and
waste ground

What does it look like?
A rather straggling and
stiff-stemmed plant

*If roasted and powdered,
the roots are used as a
substitute for coffee.
True or False?*

15 POINTS
Double with answer

Bluebell

Scientific name
Hyacinthoides non-scripta

When does it flower?
April–June

Where is it found?
Woodlands and other shady,
damp places

What does it look like?
The leaves are narrow and
shiny and surround the
flower stem

10 POINTS

44

Common Knapweed

Scientific name
Centaurea nigra

When does it flower?
June–August

Where is it found?
In all kinds of grassy places

What does it look like?
Stiff, upright stems with uncut leaves

Bees and other insects love this plant for its nectar.

10 POINTS

Greater Knapweed

Scientific name
Centaurea scabiosa

When does it flower?
June–September

Where is it found?
Dry grassland, hedgebanks, roadsides

What does it look like?
Stiff, branched stems with deeply cut leaves

15 POINTS

Yellow flowers

Marsh-marigold

10 POINTS

Scientific name
Caltha palustris

When does it flower?
March–May

Where is it found?
Marshes, ditches and the edges of watercourses

What does it look like?
Like a large buttercup with round leaves

Creeping Buttercup

Scientific name
Ranunculus repens

When does it flower?
April–September

Where is it found?
Damp meadows and roadsides

What does it look like?
The plant is tough, tall, hairy and has palm-like leaves

5 POINTS

Yellow Water-lily

Scientific name
Nuphar lutea

When does it flower?
June–September

Where is it found?
In lakes, ponds and slow-running streams

What does it look like?
The roundish leathery leaves float at the surface and the flowers are carried above them

 15 POINTS

Wild Mignonette

Scientific name
Reseda lutea

When does it flower?
June–September

Where is it found?
Disturbed ground and wasteland

What does it look like?
The bristly stems carry spikes of pale yellow flowers

The name comes from the French for 'dainty'.

 15 POINTS

Perforate St John's-wort

Scientific name
Hypericum perforatum

When does it flower?
May–September

Where is it found?
Open woods, scrub, dry grassland

What does it look like?
When held up to the light the leaves seem to be marked with pale spots

15 POINTS

Common Rock-rose

Scientific name
Helianthemum nummularium

When does it flower?
May–September

Where is it found?
Dry chalk grasslands

What does it look like?
The flower looks like a single yellow rose

15 POINTS

Kidney Vetch

Scientific name
Anthyllis vulneraria

When does it flower?
April–September

Where is it found?
Dry grassland, dunes, sea cliffs

What does it look like?
The flowers are carried in round clusters at the top of the stem

15 POINTS

Agrimony

Scientific name
Agrimonia eupatoria

When does it flower?
June–September

Where is it found?
Dry fields, roadsides, wasteland

What does it look like?
Upright, sometimes reddish stems with saw-edged leaflets

15 POINTS

Silverweed

Scientific name
Potentilla anserina

When does it flower?
May–September

Where is it found?
Damp fields, hedgebanks, roadside
wasteland

What does it look like?
The leaves are arranged in
rosettes from which
runners creep

*How did this
get its name?*

15 POINTS

Double with answer

Creeping Cinquefoil

20 POINTS

Scientific name
Potentilla reptans

When does it flower?
May–September

Where is it found?
Dry roadsides and wasteland

What does it look like?
A creeping, mat-forming plant
with long runners

*The name comes from the Latin
for 'five leaves'.*

50

Cowslip

Scientific name
Primula veris

When does it flower?
April–May

Where is it found?
Hedgebanks, roadsides, old meadows

What does it look like?
The rosette of Primrose-like leaves surround a medium-height flower stem

15 POINTS

Primrose

Scientific name
Primula vulgaris

When does it flower?
March–May

Where is it found?
Woods and banks beside roads and railways

What does it look like?
The flowers may be either pin-eyed (long style) or thrum-eyed (short style)

The plant in the picture is pin-eyed.

10 POINTS

Double for finding both kinds

51

Yellow Pimpernel

Scientific name
Lysimachia nemorum

When does it flower?
May–July

Where is it found?
In dampish woods

What does it look like?
Creeping stems in large
masses

TOP SPOT!

25 POINTS

Common Toadflax

Scientific name
Linaria vulgaris

When does it flower?
July–September

Where is it found?
Grassy places and waste
ground

What does it look like?
Like a small-flowered
garden snapdragon

10 POINTS

Corn Marigold

25 POINTS

Scientific name
Chrysanthemum segetum

When does it flower?
May–August

Where is it found?
In arable fields with wheat
or other crops

What does it look like?
Masses of bright yellow
flowers on tall stems

TOP SPOT!

Bulrush

Scientific name
Typha latifolia

When does it flower?
June–August

Where is it found?
Edges of rivers, lakes and ponds

What does it look like?
Long, stiff grey leaves and
sausage-shaped flower spikes

*The roots provide a safe place for
young fish to hide.*

5 POINTS

Lesser Celandine

Scientific name
Ranunculus ficaria

When does it flower?
March–May

Where is it found?
Hedgerows, gardens, roadsides
and woods

What does it look like?
A low-growing buttercup with
heart-shaped leaves

15 POINTS

Great Mullein

Scientific name
Verbascum thapsus

When does it flower?
June–August

Where is it found?
Dry, grassy or stony places

What does it look like?
It may reach 2 m (over 6 ft)
in height; the leaves and stem
are woolly

15 POINTS

Honeysuckle

Scientific name
Lonicera periclymenum

When does it flower?
June–October

Where is it found?
Woodlands and hedgerows

What does it look like?
A woody climbing plant with
sweet-smelling flowers

10 POINTS

Smooth Hawk's-beard

Scientific name
Crepis capillaris

When does it flower?
June–November

Where is it found?
Grassland and waste ground

What does it look like?
The flowers resemble small
Dandelions carried on tall,
thin stems

10 POINTS

Common Ragwort

Scientific name
Senecio jacobaea

When does it flower?
May–October

Where is it found?
Neglected fields, dunes and roadsides

What does it look like?
An upright, branched plant with strong-smelling leaves that are poisonous to livestock

5 POINTS

Traveller's-joy

Scientific name
Clematis vitalba

When does it flower?
July–September

Where is it found?
In woods and hedgerows, mainly on chalk and limestone

What does it look like?
A big, woody climber with fragrant flowers

20 POINTS

Goldenrod

Scientific name
Solidago virgaurea

When does it flower?
July–October

Where is it found?
Dry woods, hedges, dunes, grassy and rocky places

What does it look like?
The flowerhead takes the form of a branched spike with many tiny flowers

Dandelion

Scientific name
Taraxacum officinale

When does it flower?
Irregularly throughout the year

Where is it found?
Road verges, gardens, farmland, waste ground, fields

What does it look like?
The flower stems are hollow and contain a milky juice

Where does the name come from?

5 POINTS
Double with answer

Perennial Sow-thistle

10 POINTS

Scientific name
Sonchus arvensis

When does it flower?
August–September

Where is it found?
Gardens, farms, roadsides, waste ground

What does it look like?
Similar to the Dandelion, but with many flowers on each stalk rather than a single flower

Carline Thistle

Scientific name
Carlina vulgaris

When does it flower?
July–August

Where is it found?
Dry grassland

What does it look like?
Low-growing and prickly

TOP SPOT!

25 POINTS

Golden Samphire

Scientific name
Inula crithmoides

When does it flower?
July–August

Where is it found?
On sea cliffs and salt marshes

What does it look like?
A big, fleshy-leaved daisy

25 POINTS

Common Fleabane

Scientific name
Pulicaria dysenterica

When does it flower?
July–September

Where is it found?
Ditches, marshy meadows and damp roadsides

What does it look like?
A big, shaggy plant with masses of yellow flowers

20 POINTS

59

Lady's Bedstraw

Scientific name
Galium verum

When does it flower?
July–August

Where is it found?
In dry, grassy places

What does it look like?
Masses of tiny, yellow flowers on sprawling stems

The name comes from the fact that people used to use this plant for bedding!

20 POINTS

Wood Sage

Scientific name
Teucrium scorodonia

When does it flower?
July–September

Where is it found?
Woodland edges, hedgebanks and other fairly dry places

What does it look like?
A downy plant about 30 cm (1ft) high with wrinkled leaves

20 POINTS

Colt's-foot

Scientific name
Tussilago farfara

When does it flower?
February–April

Where is it found?
Wasteland, dunes, riversides

What does it look like?
Dandelion-like flower but the
leaves are heart-shaped

15 POINTS

Yellow Iris

Scientific name
Iris pseudacorus

When does it flower?
May–August

Where is it found?
Ditches, lakesides, riversides,
wet woods

What does it look like?
Like a yellow garden iris

10 POINTS

Broom

Scientific name
Cytisus scoparius

When does it flower?
May–June

Where is it found?
On dry, acid soils such
as heaths

What does it look like?
A small, dark green,
spineless shrub

5 POINTS

Gorse

Scientific name
Ulex europaeus

When does it flower?
March–June

Where is it found?
Heaths and hillsides

What does it look like
A spiky bush

*Some people think the
flowers smell of coconut.*

5 POINTS

Index

Answers: **P6:** Jack-by-the-hedge, Jack-among-the-hedgerow **P13:** True (but they should never be eaten raw) **P14:** Cuckoo pint **P17:** Black **P19:** Hips **P23:** Blackberry **P25:** Lady's smock **P29:** Because it grows on burnt ground **P30:** False. It is called Ling **P31:** The heart resembles a Crane's bill **P41:** From the beak of the fruit, which **P36:** Because the leaves were once used to dress wounds **P50:** Because the silky hairs make the underside of the leaves look silvery **P57:** Dent de lion (French for 'lion's tooth'), which refers to the toothed leaves

i-SPY
How to get your i-SPY certificate and badge

Let us know when you've become a super-spotter with 1000 points and we'll send you a special certificate and badge!

Here's what to do:

✓ Ask a grown-up to check your score.

✓ Apply for your certificate at www.collins.co.uk/i-SPY (if you are under the age of 13 we'll need a parent or guardian to do this).

✓ We'll email your certificate and post you a brilliant badge!